WHO

WHO WILL ROLL THE STONE AWAY?

*The Ecumenical Decade of the
Churches in
Solidarity with Women*

Mercy Oduyoye

BOOK SERIES

WCC Publications, Geneva

261.8344

Cover design: Rob Lucas

2001S436

ISBN 2-8254-1018-7

©1990 WCC Publications, World Council of Churches,
150 route de Ferney, 1211 Geneva 2, Switzerland

No. 47 in the Risk book series

Printed in Switzerland

Table of Contents

1. The Beginnings

What we need

Wherever this story is told, it will be told in memory of him.

An African Methodist bishop, a man, listened to the deliberations at a World Council of Churches central committee meeting that was held after the United Nations conference in Nairobi to mark the end of the UN Decade for women. A slide-tape presentation had highlighted the WCC contribution to that gathering. One of the delegates observed that "the churches had not been sufficiently aware of the Decade; and in many churches, the position of women has not improved in the last ten years". During the discussion that followed, our Methodist bishop declared: "What we need is a churches' decade for women."

It was certainly not the first act of solidarity with women by a "church leader" at the central committee, and the bishop was by no means the first man in this key decision-making committee of the WCC to stand firmly with women. In him we recall and we anticipate the solidarity of all who belong to the church. What we need is a decade of solidarity with women. We, the church, stand in need of it.

The Bible studies and worship at the 1987 meeting of the working group of the WCC's Sub-unit on Women in Church and Society were built around the Easter story. They specifically focused on the question of the women who ask: "Who will roll away the stone?"

The imagery of stones as stumbling blocks hampering women's lives was a fertile ground for discussion. The stream of "resurrection people" that has flowed from the empty tomb has continued to broaden and deepen. The story of the two who walked with the risen Christ towards Emmaus without recognizing him was also helpful as we planned for a journey that would take ten years to complete. Each step counts and each move has to be checked with the risen Christ. On this journey we shall constantly be in conversation with Christ who will help us to interpret the past record of the church in relation to women.

A look at the past

Women have stood in solidarity with Christ and with the church since the day Mary of Nazareth said "Yes" to God. "Behold, I am the handmaid of the Lord," Mary said to God's messenger. "Let it be to me according to your word" (Luke 1:38).

Salome and many others put their material wealth and spiritual resources at the disposal of the Jesus school. Lydia and Priscilla supported with all their resources the Jesus movement in its infancy. Through the centuries women have been ardent supporters, promoters and facilitators of community in their churches, as they are today.

What the call of the WCC is asking is that the churches respond to women's faithfulness by becoming more open to the full humanity of women and through an explicit recognition of the women the churches baptize into Christ. The WCC is calling the churches to obey God rather than conform to the norms of man-made culture. The decade is an opportunity for the churches to take stock of how woman-power functions in the church community and what women's resources the churches must acknowledge and make use of. It is a decade during which the churches are to review how much women's thinking and planning go into the day-to-day life and the total mission of the church. It is not a decade for research and documentation and publication *only*. It is a decade offered to the churches *to act* justly towards women and to be faithful before God.

The WCC has member churches which date from the beginnings of the Christian era, and are spread all over the world. It is hoped that the Decade will also touch churches which are not members of the WCC. Nevertheless, for this survey we stay with the Council and its member churches, from the reception of Sarah Chakko's report on "The life and work of women in the church" at the very first assembly of the WCC. This way we shall make an overview of the history of less than half a century. A good deal of that story has been told by Susannah Herzel in *A Voice for Women*.

It is worth noting, however, that it took seven years from its founding for the WCC to establish a department to deal with the issue of the co-operation of women and men in church and society. The first director, of the department, Madeleine Barot, brought with her a legacy of women's meetings that were held prior to the major WCC events and other ecumenical gatherings, which had ensured that women's presence was kept visible.

The story as I have known it begins only in 1967 when an African woman, Brigalia Bam, joined the staff of the World Council of Churches. She assumed charge of the then Department of Co-operation of Men and Women in Church and Society, and took the "women's concerns" beyond questions of ordination and participation in the church.

Some member churches became more relaxed as they saw the work develop along the lines of global issues of women's development and women's rights as human beings. This gradually led to the understanding of *sexism* as a deficiency in human relations and an evil to be resisted and uprooted. That was the understanding reached at a consultation on "sexism" that met in 1974.

Sexism? What has it to do with ecumenism? There were a lot of sniggers, and the churches relaxed even further. None of this was seen as threatening, for the issues were perceived as being non-theological. Not even a subsequent consultation of women seminarians was seen to be raising ecclesiological issues.

But the leadership of the WCC in this area was global and representative; it had involved an Asian, an American, a European, and then an African woman.

Sexism is indeed a challenge to the church worldwide, as it came to be recognized later.

In the beginning, the theological presupposition of an order of nature which put women a little lower than men, and ruled out their leadership when men were present and available, was the centre of thought and action and debate. Member churches of the WCC have for long accepted — if not prescribed — a variety of limitations on women's presence in the church, but together as a council they have now undertaken to dismantle these obstacles and to urge the churches to examine their traditional attitudes and practices.

Ten years before the WCC meeting that called for the Decade, the Council had embarked upon a broad-based study lasting four years (1978-81) to get its members to assess the state and health of the community of women and men in the church. The "Community study" as it came to be called generated unprecedented interest and inspired a number of groups worldwide. It identified the strands in the web of oppression, such as sexism, racism, classism and other demonic forces that divide the human community and even the churches.

The Council received the report of the Community study at a central committee meeting held in Dresden in 1981. After a long and heated debate it was decided to attempt to implement some of its recommendations as a Council. It is interesting to recall that the debate was centred on numbers. Many members had difficulty in seeing the church as made up of roughly fifty percent male and fifty percent female persons. If that was not the difficulty, then it was located in the prevalent feeling of inappropriateness. How could women sit on councils that decide the direction of what the church is about?

Whatever the real problem was, Dresden was the place where some Christians seemed to be saying that women are a stumbling block to the visible unity of the church. But in spite of all the nagging doubts and fears, there is now a decision on record that the Council will aim at equity of representation between men and women on its assemblies.

The Council has stood with women in many ways. Dresden marked a new stage insofar as it affirmed women as full participants in the life of the church. This set the Council apart from many of its member churches, and indeed over and against some of them. Naturally we cannot attain that kind of representation at Council level when churches send "leaders" and women are not "recognized" leaders in the churches to which they belong. The effort to achieve such parity in WCC meetings is often frustrating. Not even the one-third mark set for the Nairobi assembly and later meetings was an easy target to reach. Yet, as if that had been achieved, a meeting on resource sharing in 1987 recommended that the Council and its member churches should move closer to parity of representation by taking the next step — forty out of every hundred people who come together to consult on church matters should be women. Women *are* a resource for the church and their thinking, insights and issues must be appropriated by the whole body of Christ, not just seen as those of an interest group from within or a pressure group from without. Women's experiences form part and parcel of the church's experience.

Thus since its foundation in 1948 the WCC has kept itself and its member churches conscious of the fact that both church and society are doing less than justice to women, first with the concept of co-operation, and then with that of community. Now it has become aware that both these emphases must involve a call for repentance and renewal. Perhaps for too long it has been trying to promote dialogue in a situation which demanded first of all the denunciation of oppression.

The question has now been put, can two walk together unless they agree? Can we have equity of representation when women's voices are still absent from the assemblies

of churches ? With the UN Decade for Women the church
had become more aware of its role as the voice of the
voiceless. With the Ecumenical Decade now the churches
hear a call to stand by and with women as they work for
peace, for justice and for the dignity of the human as it
exists in two genders. A longer term than the four years
for study was necessary and decades were in; so a decade
of the churches' solidarity with women was in place.

The first steps

Between August 1985 and Easter 1988 steps were taken
to design and launch the Ecumenical Decade of the
Churches in Solidarity with Women. A key principle for
the Decade is that it belongs to the churches, and to the
Council is only as a gathering and dispersal point.
However, it was necessary for the Sub-unit on Women in
Church and Society, to which the Council has entrusted
the task of promoting and monitoring the Decade, to
prepare the launching pad. The "decade bird" hovering
over the ecumenical boat with the New Woman in her
beak and the future world in her womb was the gift of Eva
Saro, an artist from Geneva, to all who would be in
solidarity with women. Sharing is a central aspect of the
Decade programme, and many groups are offering their
stories to be shared around the world. This little book
brings together some of these offerings, in the hope that it
will facilitate and encourage more sharing.

The World Council staff, guided by members of the
working group of the Sub-unit on Women, offered the
"Yellow Book", the first of the Decade publications. It
deals with the purpose of the Decade in five points around
the key terms empowering, affirming, giving visibility,
enabling churches, and encouraging action and dynamic
movements. Women must challenge oppressive
structures. All who are in solidarity with women are to
acknowledge and enhance the contributions of women in
significant ways. Women's perspectives and creative life-

affirming efforts are no longer to be left under bushels of modesty. The churches must work towards freeing themselves from sinful divisions and from all that discriminates against women. Above all, churches are to act in solidarity with women — they must deliberately and intentionally stand with women for what enhances their humanity.

So at Easter 1988, the Ecumenical Decade of the Churches in Solidarity with Women was launched at the Ecumenical Centre in Geneva and in several churches around the world. For most the call came too late for the Easter date but many found space for it during that period and after. Even as I write (June 1990) a church in Uganda is preparing to launch the Decade, and it may not be the only one.

The launching has taken many forms but it was unfailingly an expression of joy and empowerment. The knowledge of participating in a global effort is stimulating. It continues to generate energy in hundreds of groups, all actively involved, in many parts of the world.

In preparation for the launching, the working group of the Sub-unit on Women, which met in India in January 1988 to help shape the Sub-unit's programme, gave a good deal of time to deliberations on the Decade. Already women in India had begun preparations for the Decade. Their meeting in Madras, in which some of the working group members participated, had an impact that reached far beyond India. The material that was drafted at the meeting developed into the small brochure now known as the Yellow Book, which has a charterlike significance for groups around the world. It has been translated into a number of languages, and in many cases adapted to respond to local needs.

The Yellow Book describes the Decade as "a WCC initiative" but it stresses the fact that "it is not limited to the Council nor even to its member churches". The work will be in the hands of Christian people everywhere. The whole ecumenical movement — councils, conferences, associations and groups, global, regional and national, in cities and rural communities — is expected to take up the issues and promote solidarity with women.

Solidarity involves linking up into a network of mutual support. It was therefore expected that many forms of co-ordinating activities would be undertaken and information concerning such events shared globally. In this way, the Decade will become a long-term framework for the many women's support groups and movements that are already engaged in promoting the cause of women and empowering people to liberate themselves. Promoters of the church's solidarity with women will have the added responsibility of ensuring that it is the whole body of the church that is at work in this venture. When that happens we will have the moral strength to call in question the practices, attitudes and thinking in other sectors of life where too women are victims of discrimination.

We also find in the booklet a clear account of the WCC's journey towards increased awareness of the churches' own marginalization of women, beginning with Sarah Chakko's report years ago to the launching of the Decade. By thus celebrating in all local churches and women's groups the milestones of gathering awareness, we stress the need to affirm women as an integral part of the body of Christ and of the human community, and not as an "interest group" seeking to be admitted into a "man's world". In agreeing to launch the Decade, the WCC confesses that the old struggles continue, that it is not true that the problems have been solved, and that the question "What do women want?" is often asked with no intention of waiting for or listening to the response.

The struggle indeed continues. The churches are being asked to continue the efforts of the United Nations (which crystallized in the convention in December 1979 on the elimination of all forms of discrimination against women) and to follow up with concrete action the issues they presented to the UN conference in Nairobi 1985. It is not enough to tell governments that "in times of economic difficulties, women are among the first to lose their jobs". It is not enough to break the silence around the links between poverty, military bases and sex tourism. The Decade's challenge is for all in the churches to come together to wipe out the evil of sexism from the teachings, traditions and attitudes of the churches.

The questions raised by the Decade are questions touching our faith as Christians. Solidarity belongs to the faith. We speak in terms of unity and community; we call ourselves families and communions. We believe that we belong together, that as the church we are one body and when one part suffers all suffer and the gift of each is the asset of the whole. We believe that the love of God binds us together and inspires our love for one another. We believe in a creator God, whose creatures all human beings are — male and female. Indeed we claim to be God's very image whether we are male or female — and in being male and female. The Decade calls us to learn afresh the lessons which the theology of creation teaches us. Not only to learn, but also to live out the consequences.

Our religion speaks of death and resurrection. We believe in the Spirit of God strengthening and renewing us to stand for life. We affirm our participation in the church which begins with our common baptism, and we believe that Christ Jesus has inaugurated a new community whose standards and values are not of this world. Love, peace, justice, caring, healing, grace and truth are words we use daily. The Decade's call is for churches to live these out.

The WCC has suggested three areas for the consideration of its member churches. They relate to: women's full participation in church and community life; women's perspectives on and commitment to justice, peace and the integrity of creation; women doing theology and sharing spirituality.

In all these areas the churches are challenged to affirm women's contributions, to unveil women's history, and to explore new ways of exercising power. In all that the church does, it is hoped that equal place will be given to women so that the churches may open up to fresh approaches in their life and mission.

We had much to commemorate, to celebrate and to uphold. The WCC therefore encouraged the churches to launch the Decade with celebration and worship at Easter 1988, making use of special worship materials, including an Easter message announcing the Decade to be read in church services and other gatherings.

At the level of the WCC a "Decade Link" was created to transmit globally what is being done locally through publications and other media efforts. Women are being encouraged to share in this multi-media enterprise. Not a few men have demonstrated their solidarity with the Decade as individuals and as church officials by contributing to this effort. The *Decade Link*, a special English-language publication of the WCC, has become the focus of the international Decade exchange, covering a wide area of offerings, news of what has been done and what is being planned, Bible studies and theological reflections, hymns, songs and prayers, and liturgies for celebrations. Through all this we find the Decade groups working on a variety of issues such as militarism, racism, events and decisions that aggravate the material poverty and humiliation of women, violence against women, the specific effects of displacement, war and prostitution. Several areas of silence such as human sexuality and domestic violence, which affect the quality of life of the community of women and men, have in this process received exposure and expression.

The concentration and the methodology of Decade involvement vary from region to region and from country to country and even from church to church. By and large the churches have recognized their need for the Decade.

Women have been empowered by its global scope and both men and women are being nourished by its very existence.

The launching took more than a year as it had to be fitted into local schedules. The local Decade is not necessarily the same as the global one. When we celebrate the mid-Decade in 1993 there will be regional dates so that together and separately we shall all be involved with churches in their acts of solidarity with women. The WCC's call is for a decade of *churches* in solidarity with women; at the end of the day the *churches* will have to give an account of what has been done and what has been achieved and appropriated.

2. The Launching

The WCC had a twofold role in the launching of the Decade. One was to encourage member churches to involve themselves fully and work towards the goals set. The other was to monitor the progress made and facilitate the exchange of information.

The Sub-unit Newsletter, *Women in a Changing World*, brought out a special issue in June 1987 on "Ecumenical Decade 1988-98: Churches in Solidarity with Women". A subsequent issue of the newsletter carried worship resources for launching the Decade, and included a poster with the Decade bird. Translations of the Decade brochure were made available in Spanish, French and German. Translation into other languages was encouraged. A resource package was produced for group study and action, including information about what various WCC departments are doing in solidarity with women. This has since developed into a periodic publication of Decade resource kits. Following a call for persons to serve as contacts for the global sharing, decade co-ordinators were designated. They are volunteers and have remained linked to the Geneva effort. Locally, structures have developed both formally through churches and councils and informally through women's networks to maintain the global sharing with and through Geneva.

The following Easter message marked the launching of the Decade:

> "And when the sabbath was past, Mary Magdalene, and Mary the mother of James, and Salome, bought spices, so that they might go and anoint him. And very early on the first day of the week they went to the tomb when the sun had risen. And they were saying to one another... 'Who will roll away the stone for us from the door of the tomb?'"

As these women of faith set out on a journey to perform an act of love they remembered the stone — an obstacle they would have to deal with before they could be with their Saviour. And they ask each other: "Who will roll the stone away?"

When they look up they find the tomb stone rolled away. And they are astonished. Yet they have the courage to enter into the tomb. It is empty. The angel says to them, "Do not be amazed; you seek Jesus of Nazareth, who was crucified. He has risen, he is not here; see the place where they laid him. But go, tell his disciples..."

At this Easter season the churches set out on a journey of faith in solidarity with women. We will encounter many stones — obstacles that will have to be rolled out of the way so that we may become a new and living community. We today ask each other: "Who will roll the stone away?"

There are practices and teachings in the churches that are obstacles to women's creative theological, spiritual and decision-making contribution in church and society. There are structures and patterns of leadership and ministry that block partnership between women and men. We ask ourselves: "Who will roll the stone away?"

We as a church must recognize that in most instances women experience the worst effects of poverty, economic injustice, racism, casteism, militarism, and suffer more than others from the denial of land and minority rights. Women are the poorest of the poor, always with limited access to food, education and paid work. Women's bodies are abused by medical technology and sold into prostitution. Women are the victims of various forms of violence. Women of the world are asking: "Who will roll the stone away?"

We as a church are not free from idolatries and power structures that oppress people. We do not always admit that we sin by creating and justifying obstacles that destroy God's purposes for the earth. We do not empower women to challenge oppressive structures in the global community, our country and our church. We as women and men are called to repent, and together we say: "We will roll the stone away."

We as the church celebrate the visions and commitment of women to the struggles for justice, peace and the integrity of creation in our wounded world. Women and men created in the image of God are today all invited to take part in the human responsibility of caring for all life.

During the Ecumenical Decade of the Churches in Solidarity with Women, we as a church will rise up and identify the obstacles to women's full and active participation in church and society. We will work to remove the obstacles. We will affirm women's perspectives and contributions. We will pluck up and break down, build and plant. We will participate with God in transforming the world. We will say to each other: "We will roll the stone away."

We will become a new and living community in Christ, a growing stream of resurrection people, a people of God on a faith journey of hope. We will be filled with the inevitable fears and doubts caused by the stones we will encounter on the way, but we will move on compelled by love. We will find the challenge of the risen Saviour. "Do not be amazed; you seek Jesus of Nazareth, who was crucified. He has risen, he is not here... but go, tell his disciples..."

Africa

To launch the Decade in Africa, the All Africa Conference of Churches called a continental conference in October 1989 in Lome, Togo, under the theme "Arise and Shine, for the Light is Come". It had as one of its objectives the identification of the emphases which need to be followed in Africa during the Decade. The circle of concerned African women theologians, which had been in formation since 1983, was inaugurated in September 1989 with the theme "Daughters of Africa, Arise". With the life-restoring miracle of Jesus as background, African women theologians face the Decade with a strong faith.

Zonal and national gatherings to launch the Decade have taken place in Botswana, Ghana, Kenya, Lesotho, Madagascar, Namibia, Nigeria, Rwanda, South Africa, Sudan, Tanzania, Zambia and Zimbabwe. Other countries such as Uganda have given indication of their intention to launch the Decade.

Several of these were women's events, and in places like Nairobi they numbered thousands, in others like Windhoek hundreds. Where Christian councils have picked up the call, the groups are mixed. Together with the celebrative events were processions, seminars and workshops around themes such as "Male and Female Created He Them", "Women for Peace", "Behold I Make All Things New", "The Integrity of Creation", "Women's Participation in Church" and "Unity and Equality in Diversity". Participants at launching events have included heads of states and of churches. There has been considerable media coverage, and the celebrations have included many cultural shows. Efforts have been made to translate the Decade brochure into concepts and language that speak to Africa.

The Evangelical Lutheran Church in Tanzania formed a Decade committee, which convened a national workshop in January 1989, bringing together the heads of the dioceses/synods, women's work secretaries, Christian education and development secretaries, laypeople including youth, government workers related to community development, and others. Indeed it was the whole church manifesting solidarity with women and taking into account the fact that the church is part of the larger society and the issues of the Decade affect the whole human community. The National Council of Churches of Kenya went directly to the basic issues that touch the development plans of governments, legal rights and educational opportunities for women. Plans were made to sensitize the churches on the need to empower women to exercise leadership in the church. In some places the launching had been woven into the annual celebration of the World Day of Prayer for Christian Unity.

In the midst of the turmoil of the bombing of Khotso House, the women's ministry division of the South African Council of Churches (SACC) produced a booklet on the launching. Nothing could dampen the enthusiasm for the Decade, for even in the midst of death there is life.

In South Africa the women's ministries of the SACC is the Decade committee. For this committee action is the key word for the Decade. Their premise is that platform speeches and recommendations have reached saturation point, without producing anything concrete or affecting the attitudes that govern people's lives. For the women of this committee the motto is "From servitude to service: A stagnant church will only breed death; so we, who are the church, must ensure that it remains a living stream."

To symbolize the Easter victory over death, a group of women cleaned up the graveyard where the victims of the Sharpeville massacre are buried. The Decade was officially launched in South Africa in May 1988, following a workshop on the Ecumenical Decade in Bloemfontein.

The Namibia Ecumenical Decade committee was chosen at a consultation organized by the Council of Churches in Namibia and Namibia Women's Voice. It works with the theme "Unity and Equality in Diversity", and has a focus on rural development. Nigeria national launching (April 1988) was ecumenical and nation-wide. It called for research into the conditions of women in both church and society. The participants had in mind such issues as customs and taboos, working conditions and ordination. In Lesotho the launching of the Decade by the Lesotho Evangelical Church became the occasion for establishing the women's desk of the church. It also provided an opportunity for women from South Africa to be present as an expression of zonal solidarity.

Asia

Aotearoa-New Zealand, Australia, India, Japan, Korea, Myanmar, Pakistan and Thailand have reported launching events, and there will be more to come. In 1988 there was a regional meeting of the Asian church women's conference which took up issues related to the Decade. In India Decade committees have been formed by the Church of South India, the Mar Thoma Church and the Syrian Orthodox Church. The executive committee of the All India Council of Christian Women is co-ordinating the activities of the churches in India. The women have embarked on a variety of Decade efforts. Questionnaires were sent to men, including bishops, and to women, to ascertain what the most crucial emphases for the Decade should be. The Decade launching has stimulated new publications. The content and methods of theological education are being reviewed, and theologically trained women have begun to assert their presence by challenging seminaries to admit women as full-time students and to take active steps to recruit them and to integrate their perspectives into theological education.

Korean women theologians have been vigorously articulating their concern for the reunification of their country. The culture of domination which has divided Korean life has been named. It is patriarchal, a mindset which favours the strong and serves the interests of the powerful. The Decade is for them a welcome framework within which to build their support for the declaration of the churches of Korea on National Reunification and Peace, and specifically the Year of Jubilee 1995 which falls within the Decade. They will ensure the visibility of women in this total national effort. The Decade was launched at Ewha Women's University in Seoul and the women's committee of the National Council of Churches in Korea has taken over responsibility for the co-ordination of the work.

In Pakistan it was an Easter morning play at sunrise, attended by over 1,000 people, that marked the launching of the Decade. Manila (Philippines) too had a sunrise service on Easter morning before the formal launching, which was supported by the National Council of Churches in the Philippines. Women found their voice and spoke out of their pain and the experience of discrimination and poverty. Persons involved in an organization called "Christian Participation in the Development of Shan, Sayah and Karan State Communities" (CPDSK) in Burma expressed their intention to be involved in the Decade by translating and publishing the Easter message. They said they wanted to show their solidarity with women and endeavour to roll away the stone.... CPDSK is a non-governmental organization working with the very poor at the very base of society's many hierarchies. The churches' Decade has already moved into other organizations.

The Christian Conference of Asia has become committed to the Decade. With the national and regional ecumenical bodies behind it, and people's movements supporting it, the Decade is bound to make an impact on Asian churches and communities.

The Caribbean
An April 1989 meeting in Cuba brought together women from Belize, Haiti, Jamaica, Cuba and Puerto Rico. They considered their needs and set priorities for meeting them. The problems that women face vary from country to country, but the root causes are the same. In the Caribbean, among their problems are domestic violence, and the negative image of women, and both result from their lack of voice in the decisions that affect them. These have become Decade issues now. The women have also called on the churches to give greater attention to the

theological education of women and to their inclusion in all aspects of the church's life.

In Jamaica, the Council of Churches held a workshop during which the Decade was projected as a means of seeking justice and full opportunity for women. Economic backwardness was identified as a reason for the failure of women and men to work together on an equal basis for the common good of the community.

Europe

By the end of 1988 several activities had been reported from various parts of Europe — Italy, Hungary, Czechoslovakia, Germany, Holland, Belgium, France, Switzerland, Sweden, Austria and Britain. In several places the Decade brochure was used widely as a basis in special issues of their regular church or women's publications.

Worship was the most common way of launching events. Easter morning gatherings of women took place over much of Sweden. The Easter launching service in France was broadcast over the radio. The Swiss had a one-hour TV programme that included the reading of the Easter message. At Westminster Abbey in London, 500 people gathered for a worship service prepared by the Women in Theology group, and the Methodist churches had women preachers in all the Easter services. Women's pilgrimages took place in many parts of the British Isles. The local Decade subject is "Ecumenical Decade — Christian women say: Count me in."

But it was not always a "women only" affair.

The Decade launching worship that took place in the Sophienkirche, Berlin, was prepared jointly by the Protestant women's and men's departments of the German Democratic Republic. Nor was the Decade left to the churches only; the Christian Peace Conference officially promulgated the Decade at its March 1988 meeting in Budapest. The membership of Austria's Ecumenical

Forum goes beyond church affiliations, and here too the Decade has been well accepted.

As in other regions, the Europeans have identified a number of important issues and set their own priorities for action. They will combat all kinds of violence against women including sexual violence; they will take up the cause of migrant and refugee women; they will fight militarism and the kind of tourism that is insensitive to culture and promotes prostitution. They are concerned about the working conditions of women such as those on assembly lines, and the manipulation of women's bodies as in bio-technology. They will encourage the study of the Bible and the doing of theology, and work for economic justice and much greater participation in decision-making.

A study of the methods proposed shows that there will be a focus on women's experience and that issues such as racism and ethnic conflicts, which have global implications, will be analyzed and addressed specifically in relation to the impact they have on women and as women see and experience them. Women's contributions, hitherto largely unwritten and unsung, will be made available to provide the role models that are so sadly limited at present. Women have played roles that have made them legendary figures, but their stories are known only to experts. Women's art and women's power throughout history, when properly publicized, will make it possible to enhance and renew women's lives at the present time.

Europe has exported its world-view to peoples everywhere, and it continues to affect other people's life-styles, especially in the south. The word solidarity, in this situation, seems to have the effect of turning European eyes to the south. In Switzerland the launching of the Decade featured an African woman. In the Federal Republic of Germany the issues identified by the Women's Commission of Evangelisches Missionswerk included solidarity with women in Namibia and South Africa and with those working in free trade zones. The emphasis on the global sisterhood of the UN Decade continues in the churches' Decade to highlight the aspect of "the ecumenical". European church women seem to want to continue this style of looking outside Europe in solidarity and identification. With global sharing, other women may well come to share the special and peculiar pains of Europe's women.

Latin America

Lively Decade groups have come into being in Latin America. The Latin American Evangelical Centre for Pastoral Studies organized a regional meeting of women from Central America, Peru and Brazil. In Ecuador it was a retreat that launched the Decade. Costa Rica, Mexico and Argentina all had women's events to mark the beginning of the Decade. Reflections on women's lives highlighted several areas of concern. Rural women, indigenous peoples, urban women, women in theological education and women pastors were identified as categories that should claim priority attention. The groups that reflected on the Decade were by no means limited to individual denominations. Also, where the launching took the form of a worship service, men and children participated. What happened in Costa Rica reveals something of the ethos of the launching in Latin America. The 160 women who met in Costa Rica to launch the Decade represented eleven denominations including the Roman Catholic Church; nine women's centres were represented; so were persons in charge of day care centres, handicraft groups, etc. Women travelled long distances to particpate in the worship service held in the Methodist church and twelve male pastors cared for the children while other men prepared the refreshment.

The Middle East

To launch the Decade, the Women's Programme of the Middle East Council of Churches (MECC) organized a meeting in Maaloula, Syria, in August 1989. Sixty-three women from different countries of the region met to set guidelines for action programmes. They analyzed their situation and identified priorities for Decade work. They plan to focus during the Decade on training women for self-sufficiency and empowering them to participate in decision-making processes; they want to work towards the goal of 25 percent participation by women in consultations and leadership training programmes of the churches locally and ecumenically. Literacy programmes for women were high on the agenda as was the production of materials to assist women to discover their place and role in church and society. It was decided to create local ecumenical women's committees related to the women's programme of the MECC and to exchange information and experiences between churches on national, regional and international levels.

In Beirut a large number of women involved in literacy education had the opportunity to come together and share experiences. In Egypt the Yellow Book was translated into Arabic.

In another event, Orthodox women from 15 countries in the Middle East, Asia, Australia, Africa, North America and Eastern and Western Europe met in Crete in January 1990 to celebrate the Decade. They wanted to make their own distinct contribution to the work that the Orthodox churches have to do to demonstrate their solidarity with women.

North America

Councils, conferences and other ecclesial and women's structures in North America received a new burst of life from the Decade call. In Canada an Ecumenical Decade co-ordinating committee was formed to stimulate the involvement of local groups and churches in the Decade. This committee works closely with the Women's Inter-church Council.

The United Church of Canada formally endorsed the Decade at its general council executive committee meeting in November 1987 and directed "the general council office, divisions and conferences to carry out a process of listening and monitoring in order to analyze, understand and take appropriate action in light of the three focal points of the theme". A conference on women and the Christian church, which took place in Nova Scotia, was nourished by themes such as "The church as an agent for social change", "Women's movement and the Christian church" and "Women's ministry to women". The Anglican Church in Canada affirmed the Decade while the Presbyterians took steps to include the perspectives of the Decade in their existing education, social action, evangelism and worship committees.

Programme officers of ten major denominations, and officers of programmes and councils in the USA constituted themselves into a committee to co-ordinate Decade resource materials for the participating bodies. This way they could begin with a "unified curriculum" while each could develop along specialized lines and with its own focus. Individual churches adopted specific resolutions to guide the Decade efforts. As a whole the following emphases seem to have emerged: study of the root causes of sexism, exploration of ways to increase participation of women in all aspects of church life and of ways to address injustices done to women in church and society. Since discovery does not necessarily imply action, those planning to work on the Decade include in their strategies plans of action on specific issues. Women suffering under sexism and racism, caste and class discriminations, will figure prominently in all Decade work.

Economic oppression and political discrimination that women suffer will also be addressed. An example of specialized areas is the Hispanic women's focus on social justice. For them the two WCC programmes, the Decade and the Justice, Peace and the Integrity of Creation process, come together as one — and women are to be empowered to be actors in both.

The Pacific

Members of the Fiji Council of Churches took part in an ecumenical women's seminar organized to launch the Decade. Among the issues dealt with were militarism, racism, sexism and poverty. The Melanesian Council of Churches held a workshop at the end of which a call was made for a churches' women's council.

* * *

At the Ecumenical Centre in Geneva, though set in the international zone, the global is also local. The community of persons from many nations employed to work for Christian agencies from Geneva is a lively worshipping community. For the Decade, it sent out a call to related groups in Geneva, inviting them to "come and celebrate with us", and on 20 April 1988 the community launched the Decade, with worship followed by a two-hour programme. The animators were men and women representing a wide range of concerns, churches, nationalities and organizations.

Central to the programme was a slide presentation based on the Easter message, followed by a panel discussion on the ecumenical Decade: its challenges to the churches/constituencies from different perspectives. There was a photo display, and posters illustrated the objectives of the Decade. Those who planned the event hoped for — and achieved — a meaningful, festive and inclusive programme. We all felt ready to begin, and to stay with the Decade.

3. Promoting the Decade

The decision on the Decade was taken by the WCC central committee in the hope that it would provide a long-term framework within which the churches could give concrete expression to the commitment that had earlier led to the establishment of the programme on Women in Church and Society. Since that action in January 1987, both the central and executive committees have heard progress reports on the Decade. These bodies, and the working group of the Sub-Unit on Women in Church and Society, have become committed advocates of the Decade. The working group constituted a Decade monitoring group to help the staff and gather information on the Decade from the regions. The Decade, then, is a programme intended to become a ground swell that is given global visibility by the Council's Geneva-based staff, the governing bodies at their sittings and by the individual members of these bodies. All who are in any way related to the WCC and all members of member churches are expected to be advocates of the Decade agenda.

Initiatives from Geneva

In planning the programmes of the WCC, the governing bodies are making conscious efforts to be inclusive, not only through the attempt to achieve fifty-fifty participation of men and women, but also in the themes and projects chosen and the people invited to pursue them.

Following the January 1987 central committee meeting, the WCC staff made a concerted effort to make the Decade come alive. The week of meetings (a bi-annual feature in the life of the staff community) that was held in May that year was planned around the Decade. Resource persons included women from the Geneva community whose contributions led to discussions on global challenges, personal responsibility and the churches' solidarity.

On the staff level, a task force on women was created to monitor the participation of women in the staff structures.

It calls attention regularly to women's concerns. An in-house Decade group has been created with fifty-fifty membership. The Decade is monitored by this group. Together with the staff of the Sub-unit on Women in Church and Society, a hearing was organized to share the efforts being made by programme units and sub-units to promote Decade objectives. Since Easter 1988, reports of events and initiatives have reached Geneva from all over the world, making the Women's sub-unit a lively, busy and exciting clearing house for what the churches have been doing and a catalyst and enabler for in-house efforts.

Such efforts have taken two forms. First, steps are being taken to improve the numerical strength of women staff persons with programme responsibilities. The staff task force on women also encourages the participation of women in commissions and working groups. It actively advocates equity in participation at consultations and on the governing bodies of the WCC. Further, it tries to ensure inclusiveness in the language used in WCC documents. The task force, together with the sub-unit, organizes events at the Ecumenical Centre to share reports on programmes that respond to the objectives of the Decade. It is hoped that general hearings of staff Decade programmes will be periodically held to help the staff to share visions and plan to collaborate where necessary.

Our preoccupation has been with setting our own house in order. Apart from that the staff has not been involved in too many initiatives from Geneva. The idea is to get the churches to demonstrate their solidarity and work towards the goals set. Advocacy from Geneva can only take the form of enabling — by way of providing information that will inspire and move churches to become less timid in their efforts and to link up with other churches and groups that have similar aims or face similar challenges.

It was only rarely that the staff had to take initiatives in the regions. West Africa was one such region. Becoming

aware of areas where there was a real need, staff visits
were made to assess what could be the way forward.
Together with local Decade groups, decisions were taken
to conduct workshops in several places and to find a way
of sharing the findings among the countries. What we had
there was a challenge to the whole WCC, not just to the
Women's sub-unit. What was called for was an
ecumenical approach involving all the programmes of the
WCC. The Unit on Education and Renewal picked up the
challenge.

A unit-wide staff group, funded by the sub-units,
planned and executed a Decade encounter with the
collaboration of Decade groups in five West African
countries: Senegal, Burkina Fasso, Nigeria, Cameroon
and the Ivory Coast. The six workshops organized in these
countries met together for five days of hearings and
strategy meetings in Lagos. It was an attempt to get
Decade groups in one area to make connections with
others, and to plan for future collaboration.

Another in-house effort to promote the Decade was
securing a slot for a deliberative plenary session at the
Canberra assembly. Participants at the assembly will
thus be exposed to the issues and methods that various
churches and groups are working with; they will have
an opportunity to discuss further strategies that may be
undertaken and new emphases that can add to the
effectiveness of Decade work. In the light of the
decision to encourage a mid-Decade assessment by the
churches, the assembly will provide an occasion to
consider regional high-visibility events to mark this
mid-point.

The central committee of 1989 approved a Decade
fund, and gave it seed money. With the many requests that
are being received, it is clear that this solidarity fund
needs to be supported in order to ensure that the Council's
support is made concrete for those who need that form of
collaboration to enable them to carry on.

Communicating the Decade globally has taken a good deal of staff time. It began with the preparation and distribution of the Yellow Book. The booklet contains discussion starters on the purpose of the Decade and a historical survey of the WCC's acts of solidarity with women. It makes clear how the Decade relates to our faith. It also gives a few suggestions about issues that have central importance in the observance of the Decade.

The regular bulletin of the sub-unit carries Decade news. *The Decade Link* was started as a supplement to it because of the volume of information reaching Geneva and the need to share this as quickly as possible.

Programme units of the council

The intentionality with which the programme units of the WCC are promoting Decade objectives may be illustrated by the examples given below. Most of these are continuing programmes but several have been recently created in response to the Decade call. Decade issues cut across all WCC concerns, and hence the Unit on Faith and Witness has undertaken several studies and actions responding to the Decade affirmation that the churches' solidarity with women is a faith issue.

At the Lima 1982 Commission meeting of Faith and Order a study project entitled "The Unity of the Church and the Renewal of Human Community" was inaugurated. Its focus is on ecclesiology. But within this, the Commission has decided to deal with two areas of human brokenness crying out for mending and renewal. One of the two has led to the continuation of the Community study and the discussion of the issue of justice. In both the involvement of women is being highlighted. There have been three international consultations dealing with the community of women and men.

In the study itself, the theme of community, especially between women and men, has been intensively analyzed, and churches are being called to move to a deeper communion for the sake of being a sign and instrument of God's purpose for all humanity. Two reports of these studies will be published in the near future. One will be of a consultation on the community of women and men held in Benin, West Africa, in 1988; the other is the result of the whole study on "The Unity of the Church and the Renewal of Human Community" which contains a chapter on the community of women and men. Faith and Order plans to continue these studies and to engage the churches in reflecting on these concerns. The Commission is preparing a draft statement on "The Unity We Seek" for a consultation of women on the ministries of the church.

One of the nine guiding principles and enduring themes of the Commission on World Mission and Evangelism stresses the participation of women and youth in the life of the Commission. In its urban rural mission, women at long last have begun to take their rightful place in programmes and decision-making structures, particularly in Africa and Latin America. A high point of the commission's work, the mission conference which took place in San Antonio, Texas, USA (May 1989) with the theme "Your Will Be Done", provided an occasion for the commission to intensify the involvement of women and young people in its work. They were affirmed as persons in mission whose witness is an integral part of the church's witness. This conference with its 44 percent women, 19 percent Orthodox and 14 percent youth was perhaps the most representative and inclusive of all mission conferences. Women's presence in such meetings usually results in new departures and fresh perceptions of reality — as was the case in San Antonio.

In the Sub-unit on Church and Society, the study on "Theology and Ethics" has drawn upon the powerful critique of patriarchal structures by feminist theologians who stress the interconnectedness of life and deplore the dualisms in much traditional thinking.

The Sub-unit on Dialogue with People of Living Faiths, collaborating with the Women's sub-unit, organized a meeting in Toronto, Canada, as a specific contribution to the ecumenical Decade. The meeting brought together fifty women from eight religious traditions. This pioneering venture is of crucial importance for the Decade. The Decade's message is not only for the churches. Other religious communities too must take a fresh look at their attitudes towards women and their teachings on the humanity of women. Issues such as scripture and tradition, authority and leadership, identity and sexuality affect women across religions. Eight video tapes of the consultation helped in sharing widely the discussions of issues at the meeting that affect women in all religious communities and cultures.

The WCC Unit on Justice and Service has undertaken both study and diakonia that respond to the Decade call. With the close co-operation of the several sub-units, issues that rank high in the concerns of women, such as economic justice for women, women's health, women under racism, and refugee women, are co-ordinated in a way which enables their presentation to the UN Human Rights Commission and to the decision-making bodies of the World Council of Churches and its member churches. At the Larnaca 1986 meeting on "Diakonia 2000: Called to be Neighbours" the call for inclusiveness was very clear. Heard often and loud was the demand that "women and youth must be given more responsibility in directing the churches' diaconal ministry". Larnaca was followed by another major meeting at El Escorial, Spain (1988), on the ecumenical sharing of resources. The guidelines and recommendations on women and youth that came out of that meeting were received and affirmed by the central committee which instructed that the recommended discipline be implemented by the Council.

The various regional desks of the Commission on Inter-Church Aid, Refugee and World Service (CICARWS) have intensified efforts to involve more and more women in their work. The Africa desk was instrumental in raising funds to inaugurate a biennial Institute of African Women in Religion and Culture, a project initiated by the Circle of Concerned African Women Theologians. The Asia desk has given priority to women's questions and leadership training. On the agenda of the round tables of seven Asian countries the Decade was a regular feature and staff are encouraging follow-up on the projects. The Asia women's network, in conjunction with regional groups, the Christian Conference of Asia and the WCC Sub-unit on Women, have created a forum to encourage the women of Asia to make an impact on churches in Asia.

Working in close co-operation with the Conference of European Churches and the Ecumenical Forum of European Christian women, programmes that respond to women's issues are on the agenda of the Europe desk. The concerns arising out of the birthing of a "new Europe" are viewed also from the stand-point of how they affect women. In particular the question of women and poverty in Europe, a much-neglected area of concern, is being highlighted.

The Latin America desk is enabling women in the region to meet and share experiences and to develop common strategies. Several projects reaching the Decade fund have come out of such consultations. The Middle East desk demonstrates solidarity with women through its emphasis on women seen clearly in the deliberations of the round-table programmes of Egypt, Palestine and the emergency programme in Lebanon. Activities are funded which serve women directly or indirectly.

The functional desks have also demonstrated solidarity. The emergencies desk, though it has no specific orientation towards women, does support women as special attention is always given to vulnerable groups which usually include women and children. Priority service to the vulnerable in emergencies is a well established principle and procedure. In rehabilitation, however, women do not come first. It is an area for study and advocacy and the desk is bracing itself to move in that direction. Refugee and displaced persons who receive the services of CICARWS include large numbers of women. In recent years much has been done in this direction with the creation of a desk for women refugees.

Together with the YWCA this desk took the initiative to create an NGO working group on refugee women. In this forum one hundred NGOs share information and advocate refugee women's issues. In 1988 they convened a major consultation on refugee women which issued a 174-page practical guide on "Working with Refugee Women". Through the efforts of this desk and those of other NGOs, UNHCR policies are specifically addressing the needs of women refugees. This effort, it is hoped, will stimulate churches and ecumenical groups who hitherto have not given much attention to the question of refugee women as a major issue. In fact, this is beginning to happen in some countries.

Two words that stand out in the language of refugee women are "fear" and "lack", both of which can be overcome with life-affirming programmes.

In Asia refugee programmes and projects designed to meet the specific needs of women have begun to function. Examples may be given from Thailand, Honkong and India. The activities include family planning education provided in the languages used in the refugee camps, vocational training and income-generating activities. The recruiting of skilled and professional women refugees to serve the refugee community has the effect of enabling them to maintain their positive self-image and encourages others not to lose self-esteem and above all not to lose hope. In Hongkong refugee women are encouraged to take up cottage industries, while in India Tamil refugees organize themselves to run medical and social welfare services with personnel who are themselves refugees. The women's committee, in addition, organizes vocational classes for the benefit of the younger women. The acquisition of language skills, a crucial factor for the integration of refugees, is a service that young women and widows avail themselves of as a means of working towards self-sufficiency during their period of refuge in India. These services go some way towards responding to the life of "lack and fear" which is the lot of refugee women.

Justice to women in the economic sphere, a Decade objective, is beginning to receive attention. The deliberations of the board of the Ecumenical Church Loan Fund (ECLOF) on the Decade led to a decision to contribute to the empowerment of women through loans and credits. Further, a commitment was made to aim at equal representation of men and women on the board. Meanwhile efforts will be made to achieve the same on the level of staff, to monitor participation of women in ECLOF, analyze the impact of loans on women's activities and to sponsor regular consultations and technical assistance in the development of women's projects. Similar policy statements have been made by the Ecumenical Development Cooperative Society (EDCS).

These decisions are in line with the recommendation that came out of the WCC world consultation on resource sharing held at El Escorial in October 1988 that 50 percent of funds channelled through ecumenical projects should go towards the empowering of women.

All these efforts mark real progress in participation. Instead of women being studied by men, some mutuality is beginning to emerge. Rather than help women through development efforts men have helped to design, the church is beginning to promote women's development through women's own efforts. Development is seen from the perspectives of women and undertaken not only through "manpower" but with the participation of women's hands, heart and intellect.

Recognizing the fact that in any situation of brokenness women suffer in a double way, the Programme to Combat Racism (PCR) has established a desk for women under racism. Pursuing this, a consultation in 1986 called upon the churches to enable increased participation of racially oppressed women in church and society and to join in demanding justice, peace and equality for women suffering because of discrimination on the basis of caste and race. The sub-unit has since then undertaken practical programmes such as enabling Dalit women of India to acquire fund-raising skills. Together with CICARWS and the Sub-unit on Women, an African women's consultation on justice, peace and the integrity of creation was held in 1989. Not least important is the data bank of women under racism, a resource to enable the women to "overcome their invisibility in the church and society". Issues taken up by PCR are, among others, physical violence and sex tourism. The publication "We the women, we the world" tells the stories of women under racism.

The "lack and fear" of women, whether refugees, racially oppressed or otherwise marginalized, is closely associated with the difficulty of having access to education and information. Lacking these, women fear to participate and are content not to assert themselves so as to avoid getting hurt. The programme of the Commission on the Churches' Participation in Development (CCPD) has directed its attention to this aspect of empowerment for participation. CCPD has held a seminar, jointly sponsored with the All Africa Conference of Churches, on women and economic justice, as part of its emphasis on women and the debt crisis. It has now appointed a woman as a consultant in this area. There have been similar collaborative efforts on women and various aspects of economic life. All CCPD networks make a conscious attempt to involve women. This ensures that statements like "Christian Faith and Economic Life" emanating from the sub-unit include input from women.

Many human development programmes include a focus on women's health. This is reflected in the work of the Christian Medical Commission (CMC). The church's ministry of healing and sharing is for the total well-being of women, young people, men and children. The emphasis on community-based health care ensures the full participation of women both as resource for and beneficiaries of the programme. The CMC collaborates with the World Health Organisation, making interventions to present the perspectives of churches and concerned Christian groups. A case in point is the call made during a WHO assembly meeting stressing the need to monitor closely the implementation of the Code on Marketing of Breastmilk Substitutes. While this affects the whole human community, it affects the health and wholeness of women and children in an immediate way. The CMC has helped to ensure the participation of women in international meetings such as the symposium on women and health held in Manila in November 1990, and has planned a focus on women for its participation in world AIDS day (1 December 1990).

The attention given to the debates on women's ownership of their bodies by the Sub-unit on Women in Church and Society takes on practical consequences as the Christian Medical Commission seeks to focus on women and health, dedicating several publications to the issue and underlining women's own participation in the processes of healing and promoting wholeness.

This survey of typical efforts of the Unit on Justice and Service points to the complementary paths the WCC has taken to promote the churches' solidarity with women — through study and reflection, building koinonia and engaging in diakonia.

The Unit on Education and Renewal reflects several of these approaches in its work with member churches and movements that associate themselves with the WCC. The programme on education has helped women to participate as resource persons in social analyses workshops in Africa, Asia and the Pacific. In family education the focus is on women's struggle for equality and liberation. Scholarship awards to women have increased by 3 percent, with 41 percent of the latest awards going to women. Small as this may seem, it is the result of a definite policy of advocacy for women, and the allocation of needed funds. A further effort is the new South-South, practice-oriented, short-term awards specially geared to women applicants. The adult basic education efforts are biased in favour of women. This programme is contributing to the strengthening and broadening of the scope of women's leadership roles. It introduces the language of assertiveness, building hope and training for transformation. These educational programmes are aimed at correcting the imbalances that we risk taking for granted. With a constituency of the poor, the deprived and the exploited, even when programmes are not intentionally geared towards women, they do attract their intense participation. The programme has begun to establish a worldwide network of resource women who can represent or participate in promoting the work of adult basic education. Women educators and women's training institutes are being empowered through the programme, while particular attention is paid to literacy for women. Both the development education and ecumenical learning programmes are staffed by women who are conscious of the need to work for the full participation of women and who consistently advocate for women and women's perspectives.

The Programme on Theological Education (PTE) has committed a sizeable proportion of its funds to theological education of women by establishing an escalating scale of support that will culminate in devoting a hundred percent of its grants and scholarships for 1992 to women. The programme is working for the recognition of women in theology and the ministry. Together with the Sub-unit on Women, a two-year experimental project for young women doing theology was undertaken to identify younger women theologians and to empower them to participate more fully in the theological and ministerial tasks of the church. Several networks of women theologians around the world have benefitted from the PTE emphasis on women, especially those in theological education since PTE focuses on training the trainers.

Spirituality, a unit-wide emphasis in the Council, receives the full attention of the programme on Renewal and Congregational Life. In its worship workshops, a considerable emphasis is placed on inclusiveness. A joint workshop on "inclusive worship" was held in co-operation with the Sub-unit on Women and the Ecumenical Institute, Bossey. The programme on Youth too responds to the Decade in various ways. On the national level special care is taken to include young women in all programmes. At the regional level efforts are made to establish a network of young women in Africa. In 1991 there will be an inter-regional meeting of young women. In its own programmes and in those of the sub-units with which it collaborates, equal participation of young women and men is the norm. The sub-unit aims to have gender balance in leadership, in the number of resource persons and even in the authorship of articles. Wherever the sub-unit calls for enhanced participation of youth it emphasizes the need for balance.

Of the Sub-unit on Women itself all that needs to be said is that all its programmes, including the emphasis on rural and poor women and its intensive participation in the Justice, Peace and Integrity of Creation process, are actively promoting the Decade. Collaboration with other programmes, in-house and outside, has enabled the sub-unit to perform the advocacy and the enabling and empowering function expected of it. The volume of information now being received, demanding to be processed and shared, has necessitated the employment of an intern.

One of the issues taken up by the Community study was "identity and sexuality". The study revealed the endemic silence around human sexuality and sharpened women's consciousness on the need to analyze and to speak out. The sub-unit followed up on this concern and fed the findings into the Vancouver assembly, which then came up with recommendations that the WCC accompany the churches in a thorough re-examination of their views and teaching on sexuality. This has received a further impetus through the Decade efforts. The sub-unit's study on sexuality and bodily functions in different religious traditions have gone on since 1983, and some of the major papers will soon be published.

The Office of Family Education too has completed for publication its analyses of information on what the churches have already done in this regard. Related to the broad question of human sexuality is the challenge of AIDS. A small staff working group has produced a pastoral counselling guide to HIV/AIDS which complements the 1988 publication of the Christian Medical Commission *What is Aids? A Manual for Health Workers*. Thus the Decade has begun to generate publications not only to communicate what is being done, but also to assist churches and persons in their pastoral ministry as they tread the path of solidarity with women.

Women and the assembly theme

This book is being written as we are preparing for the seventh assembly of the World Council of Churches which will be held in Canberra, Australia, in February 1991. The assembly theme "Come, Holy Spirit — Renew the Whole Creation" has released an abundance of energy, especially as we pursue the concerns of the Decade. The Geneva staff and WCC governing bodies are not content with merely improving the numerical presence of women at the assembly. The theme brings up specific women's perspectives and concerns, and they hope these will get highlighted at the assembly.

In preparing for the assembly, women have thought of Mordicai's words to Esther: "And who knows whether you have not come to the kingdom for such a time as this?" (4:14). But others recall Queen Vashti who refused to make an exhibition of her femininity in order to retain the luxury of her life-style.

Such multi-layered stories are giving women new spiritual insights and strength for their commitment to equity, justice, peace and fullness of life. If the churches mean business with the Decade, then when they meet in assembly women's concerns should become an integral part of their agenda. Women prepare themselves for effective presence in WCC meetings through sharing their experiences and meeting together. The issue of *Women in a Changing World* entitled "Women's Time is Women's Business Too" contributes to this process, but more important is the contribution it makes to disseminating women's thinking about, and experience of, the Holy Spirit as the power that energizes their total lives whether in celebrating or in struggling. Women see the moves churches are making towards listening and acting and they celebrate this. Women's styles of meeting, with the emphasis on community-building, identifying issues through corporate efforts, affirming one another and working towards consensus and developing together strategies for implementation are being recognized as a life-affirming alternative that builds people up while resulting in commitments that all can live with and work with.

The assembly theme calls us to a spirituality that must undergird the theology of women and men. "Lord, we did it" should be our common confession, not "the woman you gave me" did it or "I did it in obedience to my husband". It is we, the human race, that must hold ourselves responsible for the state of creation. It is we as the church who pray for the renewal of the whole creation.

Seeing the theme through women's eyes, the prayer for reconciliation becomes vividly apposite. The churches cannot speak about the Holy Spirit without praying to *feel* its movement. And to feel it, people will have to get in touch with their feelings and emotions. With this theme, the arrogance of reason and the fear of our emotions will be seen as what they are — life-diminishing and not life-enhancing.

"Come, Holy Spirit — Renew the Whole Creation" has a sense of urgency about it, but it also expresses total openness to the future and an eager expectation that the new would break in and redeem and transform the old. Sometimes going to worship service becomes for women a journey to the tomb of Jesus bearing bitter herbs — the bitterness of their lives. But prayers invoking the Holy Spirit implicitly acknowledge that we cannot imprison the Spirit. Now the women can remind the church that the Spirit comes to the whole church and bestows her gifts to each person, man or woman, for the building up of the whole community, driving us out of ourselves and our cathedrals into the streets where we can meet the people.

The spirituality that permeates women's theology, worship and protest has been expressed in poetry, prose, song and stitching, and some of these have been shared widely. So through the Decade's sharing, churches will come to hear the cry of Sarah the barren, Hagar the exiled and Rachel weeping for her children at the many contemporary war fronts.

Kathy Galloway wrote:

My heart is full of fears for my sisters
They choke my words of joy.

When we have the taste and smell of death all around us, we cannot afford to settle for mediocre solutions, says Frieda Haddad of Lebanon.

Through the Decade, women call to women, but also to the whole church. They break the long-endured silence and they burst into poetry and song: "Sister, can you tell me your name? Your own name, not that of your child or husband. Tell me your story, the story of women fighting for dignity in a world ruled by men" (Mary Sung-Ok Lee).

Out of the sense of the outrage of suppressed dignity comes the "I am a woman" poem from Africa:

> Yes I am a black woman
> I am a person with dignity
> So I deserve my rights
> Yes I must fight for them
> I must fight against all
> oppressions of any kind
> exploitation and degradation (Irene Namatovu)

Or listen to the words of Julia Esquivel: "I would sacrifice myself, no matter how many times. I am no longer afraid of death — I die a thousand times and I am reborn another thousand through that love from my people which nourishes hope." Against all odds women like Lolita Lebron of Puerto Rico still sing and smile, and those who witness it wonder and ask with amazement:

> Why do you sing and laugh Lolita?
> Is your face lit up with the joy of life?
> Are you mad, Lolita?

No, they are neither mad nor drunk. To stand up to illegitimate authority is like a resurrection from death. It is the work of the power that raised Jesus from the dead.

Speaking of this power in the assembly, the churches will not be able to run away from what it means to have women in the koinonia of the ecclesia.

The Decade calls the attention of the churches to the way the Holy Spirit speaks through the words of women and animates their being and acting. We have been reluctant to deal with the female images of God, we are afraid of emotion and enthusiasm. We hate to be caught off our guard, but when the Spirit of Truth comes we shall experience freedom, set free from all that has closed us in. Then age and colour will be of no consequence, for the whole earth shall become the face of God. This is what Frieda Haddad of Lebanon lives by, overcoming death with the love that abolishes death, praying for daybreak — the time when we shall give the earth the name of Peniel as Jacob did after he wrestled with God until the breaking of day.

4. The Meaning and the Signs of Solidarity

There are several words whose meanings we can only understand through personal experience. Solidarity is one such. I remember the time in my own life when I came to use the word solidarity from my innermost being. Solidarity is when people you did not even know existed or, if you did, you never expected to be involved in your affairs as persons, see you and say to you: "We prayed for you; we took courage from your stand." Or they contact you with messages of encouragement and prayer.

Solidarity became for me the antithesis of operating from a basis of conflict and contest. Solidarity at that time meant sympathy and various degrees of empathy. For me, it was people exhibiting ties of affection derived from a feeling of being on the same wavelength with me. Somehow these persons had entered into what I was going through and felt they shared the world-view and ideas that were prompting my decisions and determining my actions. They understood my struggle and identified themselves with me. I am sure that some of these people are still unknown to me, and some only know me by name; but I feel their presence and influence in my life very vividly. That, for me, was solidarity.

Am I in solidarity with these people? This brings us to another aspect of the word's meaning. People who support good causes do so for a variety of reasons not all of which have to do with the persons whose lives are linked with the issues or the causes. Solidarity with a human face is mutual and reciprocal. It involves elements of co-operation, rapport and sharing. It develops between and among people who are bonded in harmony. Solidarity is walking hand in hand, developing strength through unity so that common interests are protected and common aims are achieved.

To ask the entire church to be in solidarity with women is to ask for identification with the hopes and fears women live by and with, in church and society. The Decade call assumes there is an undivided church, and asks the church to care for the totality of its membership. It is a call for inclusiveness in all aspects of church life. It asks the church to live and witness in such a way as to demonstrate that its interests are those of the whole community. If the interests of any sector are overlooked the church ceases to function as one community. It becomes less than the church of Christ in which love and mutual support must be the order.

If the Decade is perceived as liable to give rise to conflict, so be it. For to register dissent over what does not make for bonds of harmony and peace is a Christian duty. Conflict is necessary, for when the common good is conceived as that which benefits only a part of the community there is no health in the body. The differences have to be acknowledged and dealt with. A resolution must be attempted so that within the body of Christ we do not work at cross purposes. If we do, it becomes "a house divided against itself". Therefore it is a sign of life to recognize the pain in the body which has led to the call for the Decade. The church is asked to be in solidarity with women because in the body of Christ the women members are in pain (as are some men) because we seem to be operating as if we are unsure whether women are fully human and therefore to be accounted responsible and accountable.

In some countries the hurt is dealt with by women escaping from the scene of their dehumanization. There are tensions and contentions in many congregations and church institutions. Discussions are polarized on gender lines. Many women are alienated from the institutional church, and many men and women are irritated by the stance of women who dare to voice different opinions. Some women are being treated as scapegoats; they are accused of "stirring up trouble" in churches. Simply because they have a different perception of their role in church and society.

Within the membership of the WCC, solidarity with women is a tenuous factor. Recommendations painfully and painstakingly made on this issue seem to apply only to the churches-in-council and not to the individual member churches. Solidarity with women means different things for different churches. That is why the Decade efforts take different forms. Sometimes one is inclined to wonder whether the churches are in solidarity with the Council on this issue. Agreements on principles do not match the practices of several member churches and often one is inclined to conclude that the Council and its members are not of one mind. Through the Decade the WCC is encouraging the churches to listen more carefully to women, and to review attitudes that prevent women from feeling at home in the church. Solidarity with women means examining why women sometimes want to establish parallel structures.

Biblical solidarity

Events in the history of the Hebrew people as they are recorded in the Bible, and the experiences of the early church as it began to spread, give us examples of what we may describe as biblical solidarity — and also its opposite, life-denying acts simply called sin. Of course solidarity is not always in support of life-affirming purposes. Sometimes it does not work in conformity with the purpose of God; it is not in solidarity with God, if we may put it so boldly. Adam and Eve agreed together on the supreme act of disobedience, daring God. Coming together to build the Tower of Babel is a striking example of solidarity. So is the family of Noah in the Ark. But while the former was undertaken for the glory of a people who wanted to make a name for themselves, the latter was solidarity anchored on the will of God. Biblical stories about the beginnings of life, like such stories in African traditions, are realistic about the competing powers of life and death.

The call for solidarity with women is a call to life according to God's will. Biblical solidarity, when it is

Joseph who became the governor of all of Egypt had brothers who were not brotherly in their feelings towards him. They had even sold him into slavery. But God used their failure in love for the preservation of the children of Israel from the great famine. Joseph met the needs of his people, a people who had no use for him but who were the people whom God had given him as his kin. Like Moses in later history, he identified with a people in trouble when he could have stayed away and disowned all relationship. As a prince in Egypt there was no need for Moses to identify with the suffering of the whole tribe; they did not even ask for it. Moses was a reluctant collaborator with God but a collaborator all the same. The vision of a promised land with a people under God's rule kept him at his task to the end. Biblical solidarity happens when people act with God to end oppression and to build new communities of freedom in partnership with God.

In the Moses story we recall the solidarity of women with women. The Egyptian midwives and the Hebrew mothers came together. An Egyptian princess and slave girls co-operated to save the life of a baby boy, who was to be God's agent for the liberation of Israel. To put an end to brutality and to rescue persons from dehumanization, God does not only perform miracles that clearly interfere with the order of nature. In the Bible more often God inspires and empowers human beings to take on the challenge.

I have often wondered how Moses felt when he came to admit to himself what must have been an open secret among the women who brought him up to manhood. Solidarity with people demands acceptance of our common humanity, our common origins as children of the one God.

A church acting in solidarity with women will be living out the Christian theology of creation and the Christian anthropology that see humanity — male and female — as bearers of the image of the one God.

Biblical solidarity may sometimes appear like an act of treason. Rahab, the woman who hid the would-be invaders of her own city and gave them shelter, cannot be considered a good citizen. She was breaking ranks, and making the city vulnerable. But bonds of friendship empower one to protect life even against one's own heritage and interests.

Friendship such as we find between David and Jonathan, Ruth and Naomi, Elijah and Elisha, is captured in the words: "As the Lord lives, your life upon it, I will not leave you." Take the case of the rape of Tamar by Amnon; "patriarchal justice" would have contrived to have her stoned as a prostitute. Her brother Absalom took her side against such injustice (2 Sam. 13). Many contemporary men have failed this test, for they do not find it easy to listen to women, let alone take them seriously. For some men solidarity with women often seems like letting the side down.

What the Decade call says is that in solidarity the only side is that of truth and justice. It demands seeing the church as one whole and humanity as a single unit in God's creation. Solidarity demands standing for the truth even at the cost of being a lone voice, standing like a Daniel for a Susanna against the guiles of corrupt judges and false witnesses.

Biblical solidarity means leading the sick to the source of healing, like the slave-girl who advised Naaman. She participated in the healing of Naaman by providing the right information (Kings 6:1-19). Sharing information in this case was enough to begin the process of change; but in the case of the man suffering from paralysis in the Gospel of Mark, providing information was not enough; those who cared for the man had to carry him bodily to the healer.

In many cases solidarity calls for lending a hand, making provision for the needy. Solidarity demands acting as the widow of Zarephath did to the prophet

Elijah (1 Kings 17:1-24); or like the hospitable woman in Shunem who looked after Elisha (2 Kings 4:8-37). Solidarity may demand of some to "let go", and to be a Cyrus to the hopes of an Ezra. When Cyrus, King of Persia, heard the call of the "Lord God of Heaven" to build for him a house in Jerusalem, he encouraged the Jews to go back to Jerusalem, and their neighbours assisted them with gifts of every kind (Ezra 1:5-11). Unlike in Babel, they were building for the glory of God, and they experienced the solidarity even of the strangers among whom they lived as exiles.

The empowerment of Nehemiah by King Artaxerxes included not only permission to leave but letters of introduction to the governors of the territories through which he journeyed. Often that is all it takes to demonstrate solidarity: enable people to pass through difficult territory.

Solidarity is not only verbal and ideological, it has to be expressed in concrete liberative acts. Solidarity is more than letting go. Freed slaves, who have no resources other than being physically alive, have a hard time being free. "Wherever each man lives, let his neighbours help him with gold... and votive offerings for the Lord's temple in Jerusalem." This is from the edict of Cyrus, King of Persia, permitting all under him who were of Jewish origin to return and rebuild the temple. Twice David was called to account for taking the side of the poor in word, while his acts spoke the language of exploitation and theft (2 Sam. 11-12:14; 14:1-24). It is no wonder, then, that those who are called to be in solidarity often resist the call. "I have never been a man of ready speech," said Moses. The solidarity road is not a smooth one, and it can be traversed only if we keep before us the ultimate aim, that of a Canaan, a land where God is the ruler of the people.

Jesus has handed over the care of humankind to the church, certainly the care of those who name his name. If the church fails, it will hear the words of Ezekiel:

"Should not the shepherd care for the sheep? You consume the milk, wear the wool, and slaughter the fat beasts, but you do not feed the sheep. You have not encouraged the weary, tended the sick, bandaged the hurt, recovered the straggler, or searched for the lost; and even the strong you have driven with ruthless severity" (Ezek. 34:3-4).

Calling the churches

One of the most difficult words to get a handle on is the word church. In the World Council of Churches, the shorthand way of identifying a church is to look at what the community calling itself a church believes. That is the criterion set in the WCC basis. "The World Council of Churches is a fellowship of churches which confess the Lord Jesus Christ as God and Saviour according to the scriptures and therefore seek to fulfill together their common calling to the glory of the one God, Father, Son and Holy Spirit."

Beyond this, of course, are the various institutional forms, forms of ministry, liturgy, discipline and so on. The churches referred to in the Decade call are primarily the 311 who constitute the WCC, but also those who are not members but associate themselves at various levels with what the Council does. The churches' solidarity with women will therefore involve a wide network of Christian churches and may include other associations of Christians who do not call themselves church. All of them have in their membership women and men. The church is not a men's club, but the Decade of the Churches in Solidarity with Women must count on men.

Churches vary in their understanding of what it means to incorporate women into the body of Christ by baptism. In some churches even the baptismal rite differentiates between baby girls and baby boys. Gender seems to be a deeply theological issue. It is a factor in the extent, form and meaning of the participation of the individual in the body of Christ.

A most sensitive theological issue for and of the Decade is that of ordination, an issue which the WCC has faced for over forty years and which continues to engage the churches. Ordination is a divisive factor and, for that very reason, one we cannot gloss over.

There is, however, an unease in some quarters that the issue, if it continues to be canvassed, will hamper the progress of the many other facets of such a call for solidarity with women. It is even feared that it will jeopardize the quest for visible church unity which was the basis of the coming together of the 146 churches in Amsterdam in 1948 to form the WCC. Can the churches afford to maintain a posture of sacrificing women on the altar of visible unity?

What then did the WCC central committee of 1987 understand by the term solidarity? The call made by the general secretary, Emilio Castro, in his letter to the member churches, following that central committee meeting which issued the Decade call, asked the churches to be in solidarity with women "in all their endeavours to promote justice in their communities and churches, and to stimulate the fruitful co-operation of women and men so as to bear witness to the power of the gospel to overcome all barriers".

The Decade is a challenge to the churches to demonstrate visibly and vividly that the forty years of WCC advocacy on behalf of women, and the many fine statements the Council has issued, are meant to change the actual life-styles and attitudes of churches and people towards women's "potential for promoting the vision of a new age in Jesus Christ", as Castro put it in his letter. At Amsterdam the churches deliberated on the status and role of women in the church, a language which re-echoes in the later UN Status of Women Commission. But the issue is deeper than one of status. It is a question of the very nature of human beings. In the church, it is the nature of the church that is in question. If, as Castro says, the church anticipates the kingdom, then we who are the church "are called upon to face the harsh realities of the anti-kingdom in history", most especially in the history of the church as well as in present realities of the position of women in the church.

Affirming the humanity of women

Solidarity with women is expressed in advocacy for issues around which women seek transformation for themselves and for the churches. During the UN Development Decade women were only co-opted into development plans fabricated by men. The UN Decade for Women went further to entrench this approach, with its emphasis on women in development. Women are now calling on the churches to be in solidarity with them as they articulate their perspective on development and as they struggle to develop themselves. The ecumenical Decade calls attention to women's development. It is a question of justice. Women are anxious to see the churches own the Decade and demonstrate solidarity with women and their search for a fuller expression of their humanity and their obedience to the baptismal vows.

Women know that there are churches that cannot accept the ordination of women into the eucharistic ministry, but will only provide for the participation of women in the life of the churches, especially in the area of diakonia. The Orthodox churches have made it clear that their support of the Decade excludes the ordination issue. It is an important caveat, but its import pales in the context in which, even as an all-male ministry, churches do not accept one another. The whole of the Christian understanding of mission and ministry is what is at stake here. The power, primacy and honour that go with being in the eucharistic ministry should be seen in the context of the responsibility to serve. "I am among you as one who serves" is a Jesus statement that applies most aptly to what Christian women are in the church.

In recent years the call to a clarity of our understanding of what or who the church is has become more and more pressing. Theologians, especially those who oppose so vehemently the eucharistic ministry of women, should be encouraged to articulate their ecclesiology. Some ecclesiastical authorities are saying that they have heard the argument from our common baptism far too often. It should be their responsibility, then, to make clear by what theology, sacramental or ecclesiological, they insist on excluding women from ordination to the eucharistic ministry. That will be a crucial contribution in the deliberations during this ecumenical Decade. The Decade is about the church; it is for the churches to state clearly where they are with women.

In this Decade women are called to unveil their true womanhood, to reinvent themselves, to piece themselves together from the bits of humanity various cultures and religions have left for them, reproduce women's own images of true humanity. In this Decade women must become self-defined human beings.

Out of the left-overs of the fabric of history, women will make a cloth of many colours. A quilt which will force both church and society to notice the variety of ways of being women. Women will demonstrate that the wonderful diversity of human character, accepted in the case of men, also exists among women. All women are not from one mould: women do not have a common eye or voice or language. Out of the poverty of women's presence in history many wonderful and creative portraits of women's contribution are coming alive.

Women's struggle for presence has gone on for centuries, and now the churches are being called to participate in this endeavour. Women can no longer be projected as "the other". Nor can they be assimilated any longer into the dominant ways of doing things in the church. It can no longer be assumed that human authority can only be exercised by men.

Partnership and power are to be seen together. The churches will show their solidarity with women when they demonstrate a new understanding of power and their willingness to share its exercise with the whole community of people. Biblical injunctions against women who teach or act in any way that requires a man to listen to them and heed their voice have to be put in their original contexts, and seen in the light of our faith in God's grace and the gifts that God alone distributes to all persons. Churches today are beginning to hear and be open to the leading of the Spirit. Sharing responsibility, sharing the possibility for acting, removing obstacles from the way of women so that they may share in the church's being and doing — all these are beginning to happen.

Partnership

Power-sharing is a prerequisite for the realization of co-responsibility. Created equally human, God made women and men stewards of creation and gave us authority to jointly fill the earth and manage it. The present state of the partnership of men and women in all cultures, on all continents and in all churches, is a state of sin. The one-sided development of the source of human authority has reduced stewardship to domination, husbanding to control, and complementarity to the paternal determining the scope of being for the maternal. Patriarchy has distorted partnership. This is what women are raising as an issue of grave implications, not only for the relations between women and men within the human community but also for the relation of human beings to the rest of creation — of miners and farmers and industrialists to the earth with its mountains, plains, rivers, plants, animals and the atmosphere on which life depends.

The Community study that preceded the Decade underlined the efforts needed to bring about just relations between men and women. Under the rubric of partnership we examined how the church community may seek ways of working for the restoration of its wholeness. We became conscious of the various ways and levels of exclusion of women, and we began to engage in advocacy for the participation of women in our collective consciousness as the church. What the Decade calls for are acts to bring about significant changes that will move women and men into fuller partnership based on the diversity of gifts given to each as an individual.

One line of action is to move towards equity in representation of men and women in decision-making bodies, which the central committee in Dresden so painfully underlined and made a target for the structures of the WCC. Over the years it has become increasingly clear that unless the member churches themselves implement this in their lives, the Council will be hampered in its own attempts. Questions still unresolved in this connection are who represents the church and who speaks for the churches. Questions are being raised that pitch numerical and qualitative participation against each other and suggest that the presence of women lowers the authority and prestige of a body and therefore that of its decisions. In this Decade we have to face our inability to associate women with authority, our manifestation of disbelief in the scripture that the Spirit of God is poured out on men and women and that the Spirit of wisdom and understanding operates in women as in men for the common good of the community (1 Cor. 12, Eph. 14).

The partnership issue goes beyond numbers, but at least presence is an index of recognition of one's responsibility to be in active partnership. We note sadly, however, that the visible, physical presence of women in the church at worship has not ensured the presence of women's experience in the determination of policies and priorities. We suggest that some of this is due to the fact that often the very language that is in vogue ignores their presence, thus making women act as spectators to the goings-on in the altar area and the board-room. The Decade calls for listening to women state their perceptions and taking them into account when decisions are made.

Participation means empowering women to become active partners in determining the quality of the life of the church as a community and of its presence in the world. Visible involvement of women in this manner is an essential element of the unity we seek in order that the world may believe.

For me one of the saddest effects of the intransigence of churches on this issue of partnership is the creation of "women churches". The women church is a challenge to assess why we are so divided. The Decade is for the churches to face the question of unity, asking and seeking answers to the questions on the role of the gender-factor in our search for the unity of the church and the renewal of the human community.

Unity and gender

The church from its beginnings bore within its body the seeds of diversity. But that it has led to divisiveness is the result of human sin. That we now have women churches is the visible expression of the deep hurt of women arising out of their marginalization. Their presence in the church is taken for granted; so is their lack of voice. Their active service in creating an environment for physical and mental health is also taken for granted. They are in the church as facilitators for the men who are the makers and actors of the church. Their silence complements men's speech. There is no unity, only a community in which one sector conforms to the forms of participation imposed upon them.

The language of deliberations on unity in recent times has taken a most unfortunate turn. Women are being portrayed as obstacles to the churches' unity as if they were not of the church. The churches will demonstrate solidarity with women, when bilateral and multilateral deliberations purporting to seek the visible unity of the church admit women's presence and serious discussion of the points women raise. Women, both in church and in society, are challenging their marginalization because it visibly disrupts the unity of community. Churches such as the Lutherans in Tanzania are responding by taking positive steps towards the ordination of women into the eucharistic ministry while the Orthodox are reviving the ancient diaconate order as a ministry in itself and not necessarily a step towards priesthood. In Africa the media are beginning to pick up the issue of the ordination of women.

The experimental project of young women doing theology and the various associations of women theologians being supported by the Programme on Theological Education, especially in the third world, have highlighted the inescapable link between doing theology and living one's daily life. They have also unearthed the socio-cultural biases against women doing theology. Christian theology is not univocal; it cannot be whole or complete if it is carried out by male voices only. The same can be said of all areas of life. In this as in any other issue, gender has been a negative factor in the search for visible unity. The Decade is pregnant with the possibility that gender will become a positive parameter, and that the WCC programmes that promote women's voices and actions will stimulate member churches to own the Decade and its objectives and to make their solidarity with women more visible.

In society women ask for reciprocity as a sign of true unity; they ask why a wife should need a husband's signature to buy land when the husband does not need the wife's signature to do the same. The unity of the church as of the human community becomes a reality when women are recognized as legal and economic and *sacramental* agents.

Causes for concern — and signs of hope

What the women of the church have done is, of course, an integral part of the churches' effort. How have the churches as institutions responded?

The Community study (1978-81) attempted to call the attention of the whole church to a more integrated way of viewing itself. It underlined the fact that the Christian community is made up of women and men. Genuine efforts were made in many churches around the world to have men and women do this study together.

The Decade has the same aim. It follows up on the Community study, in that it is asking for action on a few of the issues raised during that study. The target group is the same; men and women of the church together. What has happened since the Decade was launched?

The most widely publicized church actions have been those that militated against the spirit of the Decade. Archbishop Runcie and Pope John Paul agreed that the ordination of women would prevent the reconciliation of church families long separated over other reasons. That hit the headlines. The provincial synod of the (Anglican) Church of the Province of Southern Africa could not get the two-thirds majority needed for a positive decision on the ordination of women. That too got the attention of the press. But even in these churches there were men who voted for the inclusion of women and we need to acknowledge that they too are of the church. Also of the church are the women who are against the exercise of power by women and who create associations to oppose the ordination of women. In Taiwan the opposition to the Presbyterian churches' Decade plan was led by a few ministers and some women. The ministers took a legalistic approach, saying that the general assembly had not officially approved the Decade. They feared that through the Decade women might seize power in the congregations. In addition, some ministers' wives were unhappy; they were afraid of losing the authority role they play in local church women's groups. A report from South Africa indicated that some church women's organizations are uneasy about the Decade.

Meanwhile Eastern Orthodox church delegates and advisers, seventy of them, met in Rhodes to deliberate on and to "theologically ground the impossibility to ordain women in the Orthodox church". Yet even here one of them could say that "any act which discriminates against women and men on the basis of gender is sin", and would call on the church "to offer before the world the dignity of the human person, created in the image and likeness of God".

When we talk about this issue we should remember the many churches which ordain women, including the church in which Barbara Harris is a bishop. The Decade calls for sensitivity from both sides.

A word on church women and the Decade is necessary. The question here is not content but process. Church women's groups have been at work for many years on one or another aspect of the Decade agenda. In almost every case they have been the ones to launch or to advocate its launching. In many countries, however, the question has been how to make this a decade of the churches and not of women only. Naturally, some women's groups hesitate. In a number of places it is evident that left to the church's way of organizing itself for action, not much will change in a decade. It is also the pattern that even churches that are willing to move have only begun to take steps to empower women "to get on with it". Take the case of the appointment of co-ordinators. All are women, for it is acknowledged that women are in the best position to articulate what the Decade stands for. However, if there are committees guiding the process and the programmes they must be seen to reflect the whole church. If this is done, church women's groups will, as in India, have no fear of losing ground. They will be the catalysts for making an in-depth impact on the church as a whole.

Here, too, we must be sensitive. Church women's organizations, like churches, have their own peculiarities. This the advocates of the Decade have to bear in mind as they seek solidarity.

Several World Confessional Families have taken significant steps to promote the aims of the Decade. The World Alliance of Reformed Churches and the Conference of European Churches have both voted during their recent assemblies to establish offices for Women in Church and Society and for the Decade. The Lutheran World Federation (LWF), which has had one for some time and has worked to achieve a high visibility for women in all its structures, has taken a decision to promote the Decade and to do so ecumenically. One concrete step taken by the LWF is the establishment of a Decade fund. The LWF assembly of 1989 enabled the federation of churches to review the significant changes that have taken place since the 1984 assembly at Budapest. Changes that have been favourable to women of the Evangelical Lutheran Church in Canada, for instance, include the programmatic focus on the feminization of poverty, the development of inclusive language guidelines and their endorsement by the national church council, and the establishment of the bishops' consultancy committee on women and men. The national church council also collected and published stories of women who have felt excluded from the church.

The Evangelical Lutheran Church in America (ELCA) has created a new element in its structures, a commission for women with its own board and staff and a mandate "to assist the whole church in addressing sexism, advocating justice for women and working towards the full partnership of women and men in their participation in the church". The church has created this unit to stand alongside its existing Women of the ELCA whose constituency is the congregational women's organizations. This is an example of how a whole church can demonstrate solidarity while the existing women's group plays a monitoring and advocacy role towards the same end. It is the commission for women which is charged with promoting and monitoring the Decade.

At its Budapest assembly the LWF had resolved to work towards gender inclusiveness. It requires that 50 percent membership of elected councils, boards, committees and other organizational units should be women. The 1989 assembly of the LWF had 43 percent women delegates. Half of the main speakers were women. We rejoice with the LWF and pray that the Lutheran example inspires other churches. One of the LWF member churches, the EKD, discussed a proposal to fill 40 percent of its senior positions with women and to appoint a women's rights representative to work in the EKD main office.

In April 1988 there was a planning meeting for a worldwide Anglican gathering of women and men sponsored by the Anglican churches of the Americas. The gathering is scheduled for 1992 and it is hoped that it will be of the whole Anglican communion. This will be an important part of the effort being made by Anglicans worldwide to participate in the Decade.

At the 1990 meeting of the ecumenical Decade monitoring group of the WCC Sub-unit on Women in Church and Society, several reports spoke of the efforts being made by churches and councils and women's advocacy groups for such changes. The Pacific Conference of Churches, for instance, has a five-year plan of programmes in three areas, Melanesia, Polynesia and Micronesia. The Uniting Church of Australia has appointed a part-time co-ordinator and planned a national conference to follow up on a report on the status of women which they have in hand.

The WCC member churches in North America have all drawn up their Decade plans. In order to have a national profile these churches have formed a joint US Decade committee, and the National Council of the Churches of Christ (USA) will make the Decade its theme for study in 1992. The same goes for the Canadian Council of Churches. An example of individual church efforts is the series of ten documents on Decade issues published by the American Baptist Churches. Other churches too have initiated special Decade publications. The United Methodist Church has decided that all its committees will evaluate their work in the light of the Decade objectives, and to recommend in their seminaries the teaching of a subject called "Men Working in Solidarity with Women to End Violence". The church's financial planning includes earmarking resources for the enabling of Decade initiatives. The Decade has provided occasion for ecumenical collaboration such as the coming together of the Black Methodist churches to launch the Decade. Further, ecumenical committees have been formed in most regions of Canada to pursue the Decade objectives.

Putting the emphasis on churches' solidarity, one is inclined to say with the Australian sisters: "Thank God, it is a Decade." There is high hope that the churches will see themselves more and more engaged in doing justice to women and to the integrity of the nature of the church. Church Decade committees, church Decade publications including study materials, women and men sitting together to set the agenda for councils and synods, men being invited to church women's meetings and men's groups to review women's roles, deliberations on the Decade in church councils and synods, making budgeting provisions to work on the decade, launching and re-dedication services — these and many other efforts are indications that the churches take the Decade seriously and are searching for ways of responding to its objectives.

Celebrating the International Day for Solidarity with Women (8 March 1990), morning prayers at the Ecumenical Centre were led by male colleagues. Below is an excerpt from the prayer of a male colleague, expressing the sense of celebration, gratitude, confession and commitment. It is for me an indication of the struggles men are going through as women ask of them a re-orientation of attitudes and outlooks that demands radical re-thinking of all their relationships and assumptions. Ghassan Rubeiz, an Orthodox layperson from Lebanon, prays:

> Our Lord, today we men have to confess our sins against women. We acknowledge the structural barriers which our societies all over the world erect to oppress baby girls, female children, young women, adult women, middle-aged women, old women, all women. Barriers are created which stop women from realizing themselves, achieving their ambitions, having their dreams fulfilled, and often denying them room to dream positively and far enough.
>
> We men confess our conscious or unconscious tactics to delay women from reaching their goals, from receiving their fair share of rewards — getting sufficient education, being free, being able to express their choices about their bodies and their life-styles, creating their own designs, leading, composing, getting jobs, being what they want to be.
>
> We men recognize, painful as it is to do so, that we often take women for granted; we think of them as being ready for ever to serve with humility, for ever patient and docile, always prepared to sacrifice, always anxious to care and be kind.
>
> Forgive us, dear Lord, for taking women as constants, as formulas, as statues, as dolls, as icons, as samples, as models, as parts of a puzzle we have created.

5. Ten Years Hence?

The WCC had identified three broad areas where the churches' solidarity is urgently required. Built into the plans is the expectation that member churches will work with their own priorities and undertake what is most urgent and relevant in their contexts and for the society which they serve. When the Decade monitoring group reviewed the progress, it listed several issues that the churches and women's groups worldwide are concentrating on. No doubt by the time the mid-Decade regional events take place in 1993, more will be added, and the results of further work done on the issues listed below will be reported.

What is at stake?
In all regions there are issues related to the physical and psychological welfare of women. These figure under the title "Women and Health", and include concerns such as violence against women, sex tourism, domestic violence and traditional marriage contracts that treat wives as inferior partners. They include also human rights violations that entail a double oppression of women. The absence of women's contribution in formulating the laws of countries is a serious concern. Militarism, economic injustice, etc. affect all, children, men and women. However, given the present order of things, the state of women migrants and refugees is aggravated by the prevailing sexism that adds to the indignities that women suffer.

Physical and psychological health depends also on one's economic situation. The fact that women are getting economically poorer even in rich countries has resulted in giving special attention to the "feminization of poverty". The global debt crisis in particular is on the agenda of many churches and women's groups worldwide. Even in rich countries, resources on justice issues, especially in relation to women and children, are not easily available. How to secure enough money to carry on the Decade

64

programmes is a challenge even to women of Europe and Japan!

The psychological and practical consequences of illiteracy, and the generally lower level of women's formal education are on the Decade agenda. The low percentage of women holding political offices is comparable to that of women in ecclesiastical offices. Apart from cultural factors, both have roots in the lack of education appropriate to the offices. Women in many parts of the world have internalized their state of "sub-ordination", and are living uncomplainingly with low self-esteem, and in silence, apathy, and with servile attitudes to men and to the structures of church and society. It is a mark of the Decade that the role of men in all this is debated and put on the agenda, as is the mobilization and integration of men into Decade goals and actions. The Decade calls upon men to hear and obey the voice of God telling them to stand by the women who have chosen to obey God.

The Decade in solidarity with women calls upon the church to listen to women and to take their concerns seriously as being integral to the human search for life in all its fullness. On the agenda of many Decade groups are the issues of racism, militarism and militarization, the health hazards of nuclear testing and the dumping of nuclear waste. The exploitation of creation and the need for ecological wisdom preoccupy several groups. Issues of justice, peace and human survival and those of the survival of the rest of creation are seen as one package.

Some Decade groups have found it helpful to work with the concern for justice, peace and the integrity of creation in order to obtain a holistic approach and context within which to express the churches' solidarity with women. A programme which typifies this approach is the work by and with indigenous women in countries where Western culture alone is assumed to provide the desired ethos. Another contextual approach to the same issue is the focus on rural women, and women in shanty towns and others seeking to eke out a living from the crumbs that fall from the tables of the rich in cities. Working conditions of women continue to be a source of concern. So is the lack of appropriate technology for house-keeping and in other primary occupations of women.

Decade groups have stressed that in many countries it is religion as a whole that is the context of the solidarity women require. Where there is religious fundamentalism, women's traditional place and roles are curtailed in ways that seriously limit possibilities of personal development. Women are accused of violating traditional norms of the community when they seek to assert their individual wish to grow in non-traditional roles. All religions tend to do this with women; women's spiritual heritage is circumscribed by what fundamentalism allows. The entrenched sexism in religion is hard to tackle. Women need the solidarity of men to review the whole area of human sexuality and its links with religion, rituals and taboos. Decade groups have it on their agenda to challenge institutionalized sexism in the churches' structures, ethics and theology.

Sayings and doings

The emerging trends are encouraging. On several of the issues identified one observes efforts to speak out and to act for change. The most visible area is the empowering of women to move the church into action. Women are saying clearly that this is the churches' decade and the whole church must be working on the issues women have identified. The need to create and fund church offices to promote and monitor the church's solidarity with women is being met. Existing women's councils and committees are being strengthened. Church Decade committees are being created. In many places women have taken advantage of this to take up research and write women's histories and on women's contribution to the mission of the church which remains unrecognized. Church women are consciously linking up with women of other faiths and secular women's groups on issues that affect society as a whole.

Several publications have come out of this new burst of creative energy and empowerment — newsletters and bulletins, theological works, stories, songs and poetry, worship and other resource books, calendars, journals and brochures. There have appeared photo stories and video presentations. Methods of communication vary to suit target audiences, and drama, posters, cartoons and banners find their place alongside the books coming out of more systematic study and conference papers. Bible studies range from analytical works to group and personal reflections. Language has become a critical issue, and monolingualism is often challenged. Translation is accepted as a necessary way of respecting differences.

Structures for Decade work are many, but most common are small committees, either mixed or of women only. Several types of women's groups cut across national and denominational affiliations. Where limited to a locality or church, the groups are often linked together forming a solidarity network that is both empowering and inspiring. To keep the issues before the churches some groups have undertaken letter-writing campaigns, each with its own target groups and specific issues. Others send out carefully formulated questionnaires. Story-telling has enabled many women to find their tongues and to give voice to what they have suppressed for years. Much mutual support and counselling has developed as trust and awareness have grown not only among women but across gender lines. Exchange programmes for women are developing between North and South, and plans are being formulated for South-South encounters.

High visibility events keep the Decade ecumenical as they often demand the collaboration of several groups. Launching and re-dedication services provide occasion for whole communities to celebrate the Decade, take stock of how far they have come and to set measurable goals for the next period. Seminars on topical issues attract both men and women. A further development of this kind is the move to get Decade issues on the curriculum of theological seminaries and to remove the barriers to theological education for women. Theological works by women are contributing to creating the awareness in official church structures that the church can no longer afford to silence women. Some groups make it a point of celebrating women's gifts — launching their books, publicizing their contribution to academy, church and state, and ensuring that wherever and whenever the church speaks, it speaks also with the voice of women.

There are struggles, but the outburst of creative energy, if sustained, will yield significant results during the Decade. It is true that some churches are still biding their time, hoping the challenge will go away. For some women the goals are too many and therefore confusing. For others the goals appear vague, but for those who attempt to contextualize them, there is never a doubt that changes are needed in church and society and that the present state of women in both is less than just. It is a struggle, trying to reach the churches with this reality. The awareness percolates from global to national structures, congregations being the slowest to attempt new ways of involving women in the church's work.

It is also not easy to get a full picture of how far the churches are prepared to own the Decade. Maybe by the mid-decade it will become clear. None will be surprised if there is a backlash. On the other hand, with the visible and energetic participation of convinced churches we are assured of much progress. Justice must not fail.

And, at any rate, the church of Christ cannot afford to do other than seek justice and act in compassion.

Anticipations

At the end of the fifth decade of the WCC's life, its ongoing work on the churches' solidarity with women will be evaluated. Will 1998 be a year of jubilee for women in the church? What will be the parameters for the evaluation of achievements?

The Community study of 1978-81 focused on the issues of identity and sexuality, the roles of scriptures and structures and the challenges of inclusiveness as a principle of community-building. Since then, the increasing impoverishment of women, violence against women including sexual harassment and the peculiar problems of women under racism and in conditions of displacement have been added to the agenda. In the Decade 1988-98 we seek justice for women, to dream "bold dreams" for a new community, and to act both locally and globally for the conversion of church and society towards the recognition of the full humanity of women.

On the conceptual level my expectation is that the churches will come to demonstrate to the world community that religion is an integral part of human life and that it is an inescapable element in our understanding of society, and therefore in the struggles for justice and peace. And I hope the Decade will raise the awareness that a society's attitude towards women is directly related to its understanding of what it means to be authentically human and truly religious.

For the church this is crucial. Human dignity is no other than the respect due to the image of God in us. The Decade calls the churches to come clear on what they really believe is the nature and purpose of human existence. Should some human beings be treated differently from others — and differently from what God wants them to be?

* * *

Let me end with a well-known story.

A young woman preparing herself for marriage is confronted with a most unwelcome message. She is to become pregnant before she begins her married life. It is totally unexpected, and deeply embarrassing. The shame of it will be enough to kill her. She is being asked to do what is wholly against her religious tradition and social upbringing. She is to sacrifice her social standing and expose herself to society's disapproval. She is being asked to put the plan of God above her social and religious expectations. Who will believe that what she is carrying is of the Holy Spirit and that her act of obedience will profoundly affect the history of all humanity? Against all conventional wisdom she says "yes" to this plan of God for her.

That young woman, Mary of Nazareth, has gone down in history as the Mother of God.

What about the man who is to marry her? He stood by Mary because he too has heard the voice of God and he too believes that Mary's submission to God's purposes will bring new life to the whole human community.

Joseph too is going against custom and tradition when he takes a pregnant woman for wife. We never stop to think how embarrassing his own position is. What will his parents say? What will his friends say?

Here is a man who stood in solidarity with a woman he loved and trusted. A man who had an ear tuned to what God is saying to him and to the world.

Does the story have a message for us?